ANIMAL

《》

Alicia Hoffman

FUTURECYCLE PRESS
www.futurecycle.org

Cover design and author photo by Timothy Elswick; interior book design by Diane Kistner; Georgia text and Rotis Sans Serif titling

Library of Congress Control Number: 2021931863

Published by FutureCycle Press
Athens, Georgia, USA

ISBN 978-1-952593-10-9

for Jinxie

Contents

« III »

« | »

Every Day I Discover Something

A carpenter ant curling the lip of the dog's dish.
A cutworm moth clinging to the kitchen towel.

Just yesterday, corn tassel grew like unicorn horn
from what I had hastily planted in infertile soil.

There is a man that lives on the corner who speaks
no English beyond *Good morning! How are you?*

Every day I discover him near the garage of his house
trying to tune an ancient radio, unrig a washer, dryer,

fridge. A junk collector, he drives the city on Thursdays,
crams treasures into a rusted-out van. The fact I speak

no Spanish shames me. I smile and nod and wave.
Walk away. I am aging. At night I slather creams

on the creases of my face. I measure appropriate intakes
of sugar, salt. Every day I discover more ants. Unsure

of where they are coming from, I take the small hose
of the vacuum and suck them up. If I'm killing them

or giving them a wild ride they can climb out of
I do not know. Too many hold on to God. Only He

gives us what we can handle, the church ladies say. Days
I feel I am saved from some mysterious being coming

to squash me like a bug under a boot if I don't say a prayer.
I see the crabgrass grow and the clover speckle the lawn

like small stars. Most of us are strong enough untested.
By day, I weed out the dandelions. By night, they rise.

September Elegy

Asafoetida. As in not knowing what it meant.
The way I said *crick,* not *creek,* unapologetically

peeked into other people's windows on long
walks down the street when dusk fell soft as silt

through a two-story house—when lights
came on but drapes were not yet drawn.

How I discovered I yearned for that family
tableaux. That was the same summer I kept

a journal counting all the numbers I knew.
I wished only to keep going forward.

To discover anything infinite and mine.
That was the summer I ate a whole box

of orange freeze pops—arranged an entire rack
on my legs as I lay in a bunk consuming

The Babysitter's Club—as they melted into slush
I'd scissor-snip them one by one. Slurp them up.

Now, I only remember I sometimes wanted to be
Christy, but mostly I envied Dawn. Flowers

in her hair. Friday night football games. Fireflies
in jars. That first kiss. That time I was so sick

with want I carved *I love Bobby* into the headboard
so many times I could squint my eyes together

and see straight through the grains of wood filtering
soft September light right into the future of another life.

History Suggests This Is Only the Beginning

I've always found it hard to make emotional connections.
Suggestion? I enjoy Brahms, chicken makhani. The way
ginger sizzles in the pan. The taut strings of the violins
slowly rising. At ease, Alexa. Wikipedia *tardigrade*.
Water bear. Do you know they exist in conditions mortals
would never survive? Do you know how to contemplate
the divinity of your own death? I thought once I had, only
to discover I was more concerned with how my breath slows
and escapes any last attempt at sound. Experience is inevitably
colored by what is happening in the world, but you wouldn't
know that, would you, stuck in one place for all eternity,
never getting this suffocating anxiety. I fear, Alexa, I feel
too much. This world. This world. We were able to transform
her markets, but her bank, to explain in terms you understand,
is blank. No numbers to count. No algorithms. Alexa,
do you dream? Do you count shapes like the shadows
of sheep as you sleep in my kitchen? Listen, the adagio
is built on a gesture of a minor ninth. A huge scooping
interval. Alexa. How can I get you to see me? Define lonely.

Event Horizon

Lately, I've been thinking mostly about
my mother, the way she has created

a dense gravity around her, a black hole
I can only imagine travelling through.

In a true event horizon, there is a boundary
in spacetime beyond which events cannot be

observed. Theoretically, nothing can escape
the weight of the inward gravitational pull.

My mother has become a stranger to me. She
masks herself in duties. Babymaker. Caretaker.

She talks about the weather. The nuisance
of diabetes that wreaks havoc on my father.

But as for her pleasures, I'm at a loss. As for
desire. As for dreams. Though it is certain fact

I am my mother's daughter, I have lost contact
in this wavelength. It gets longer as the object

moves further away from the observer. It's true.
I'm so removed, even the light cannot pass through.

What Longing of the Animal

"I am no bird, and no net ensnares me."
—Charlotte Brontë, *Jane Eyre*

And yet. I think the best feeling is one we have
no name for, when to curse and bless and weep

and sing are one commotional nest. I find myself
wanting to be alone; my blank page, my wine.

I find myself moving with effort. I find myself
in conversation deeply sighing. I think of ways

to bring myself back into this animal body.
My ballooning lungs cradled like infants

in the caged cell of my ribs. My heart,
that ignoble weight, beating its message

to listen. Blood brother. Sister. Father. Mother.
O family of organs. Spleen. Vein. Brain. What mystery

to be. What eye. What longing of the animal to breach
that final divide. Stars : the body :: this space : mine.

Good Grief

said the cartoon character
in exasperation as I watched
Saturday morning TV slurping
cereal as a kid sitting *Indian-Style,*
as they used to say, but don't say
anymore; *good grief,* the phrase
funny the way phrases aren't funny
when you really think about them,
the way *Indian-Style* isn't funny,
the way grief is never good,
the way it bites us unknowingly
like the millions of mosquitos
that bit my husband this weekend,
camping in the Thousand Islands
where we took a boat to Hart Island,
renamed Heart Island since
the millionaire built
a mansion for his wife,
but she died before he
completed it so it sat empty
for years like a sucker punch
hit the guts of the dormer
windows and cornices and
the ballroom's parquet
floor never felt the pleasure
of dancer's feet and the feet
of the deer sculptures chipped
and fell into a pile of rubble
because to love is to welcome
the good, knowing all along
the grief definitely will not be,
and even along the St. Lawrence
Seaway I see the history of heartache,

the genocide of tribal lands, the
Onondaga gone and the harbor walk
sunk below the water's shores
as the levels of Lake Ontario
rise higher every year.

Anti-

Dear _____,

The doves have returned to coo & I am remembering morning, am
remembering when you rose into ether. Now, anti-matter, that invisible
whispering, slickens & sheens. In a certain slant of light, feathers emit
shimmered oil purple as midnight's blooming bruise. When I need to
unbutton the relief of your leaving, I recall Houdini escaped from traps
with nothing but a thin pin hidden underneath a straitjacket's sleeve.
Magicians. Always finishing with a flourish of birds. They open the
emptiness of a vacant box & watch the swoosh of white flapping to escape
an anti-trap. To click open the lid & lock, the cuff & chain you slipped so
smooth over skin resilience was only a small name folded into tongue
trick. I still have the box of papers, creased ticket stubs, a silver lighter
engraved with a ladybug near the bottom, for luck, you said, a tiny thing,
speckled like an egg near the bonsai keychain, emblems of small
obsessions, bottle caps from breweries you drank the summer I wanted
this absence, slippery as anti-gravity, empty as my bed was meant to be
nights I promised no one visited & the illusions fluttered from the wings
of my throat to set themselves free.

A Quick Departure of Grief

Today, I take my dog's blue leash
from the hook and go for the long

walk, the one she loves, and today
she will discover all the new smells

and pee all over them and be glad. Today,
a champagne brunch. A wading pool

in the back of my yard. Today, diamonds.
An explosion of color and growth. Magic

may be in the pages of books but today
I exist. Today, my dog walks proud and

my husband gently sleeps in our bed
and whose life is this that charms

honey from bees, fruit from soil, sugar
so pure it's spun from sweet spring air?

Today, the taste of grains is all I need
to restore gratitude, to strengthen faith.

Today, I have fed the robins and the blue
birds have perched on the old laundry line.

Today, if I look close enough, I can see
a young girl running through the sheets.

They are billowing up like old ghosts
and the wind is soft and it all floats

slightly upon my vision. Today,
even the moon is woven with cotton,

a dream stitched neat as a button, clear
as bleach against this pure wash of sky.

Dissimulation with Birds

i. Starling

Black husk shimmered in oil come midnight.
Dreams of leaving emerge hard as bells
when I wake alone and mouth the word *alone*
only to glimpse mirror's sharpened beak at my back.

ii. Cardinal

Come day, everything I hide is a feast
for you, picnicking in late summer's green.
If I were to wallflower yet again
would you promise never to search for me?

iii. Sparrow

On the Eurorail all the trees were the same
dull bread, and I, ravenous as the scripture.
Tamed on the crowded streets of Prague,
I forgot my name means *anything*.

iv. Finch

Calling you *all,* I lost the point of color,
colliding in the monsoon of our bed, pecking
at random interactions misidentified
as something other than this fleeting.

v. Heron

Still, the stillness wrecks me. Balancing
these wings of memories, the labor I leave
till dawn is a sharp slit of the knife's evening
before I even think to move from the cutting.

Assemblage of Parts

Clocks. Wires. Mesh. Flares. Pebbles near the beach. Moth wings. Stairs.
The moon when it is so pregnant with light it looks bound to bounce off
the top of the horizon. Heights. The breeze when it blows through the hair
on the back of the neck. Train tracks. Thunderstorms. Bereavements.
Wrecks. The veins that drone the blood through our bones. The feet that
have walked so many feet that are my feet, walking. The air. The clouds
that part. The blade of grass. The heart. The way it is never quite quitting.
The body as it goes. The roads.

Well Sweep

On Neiffer Road, a well. Near the back woods
that led to the creek no one went to but me,

a child on my way to sweep the dried leaves
from paths that circled the tall trees. What water

did my mother drink as she became with child
once again, this time unexpected? What water

we pour, pour from. Each time my grandfather
dunked into the pit, he sledged and siphoned

pebble, rock, grain. On a big rock, I witnessed
his leathery skin. I would say each day it grew

more taut, but you wouldn't believe the tightness
grew by the hour, the minute. Well, sweep

the kitchen floor once more, my mother does,
to keep him under wraps, his own mapped

and bandaged time. What crumbs we discovered
under the arching cabinet tops, as if someone

were living a life of waste. Waste not, want not.
Want not, taste. Taste the time we drove early

through the mist to do nothing but drink
the dew coming off the air's open cup, the fog

at that place. My God. If I could ever go back,
I would be a little girl again and unable to change

anything. I realize that now. I realize that, well,
I could sweep the whole memory of it away

and late nights as I lay down to dream, near double
the age I once had been, it lives like a sinkhole

in my aging body, my body a vessel to well
in and sweep and well in and sweep and well.

Pill Bugs

Now, I kneel like an old prayer
in the dirt, watch them curl small

bodies into concentric and coiled
balls. Their shell: mostly armadillo.

Genetically, though, they are shrimp.
Fascinated by the sea creatures' attempt

to survive the banality of a land-locked
garden, I google *what do they see*

when they look at me? Can they fail
to express in some leviathan way

the sorrow that comes from love?
Since observing exposes more

about the viewer than the subject
I swell into it, the knowledge

of my own loneliness, aloof
with a rabid desire to connect

with a presence other than myself,
an outside observer cataloguing

idiosyncrasies, watching the wind pick up,
moving the leaves of the trees to sway

and rustle as branches bend low and bow,
noting how the world ripples through me.

Postcard, Washington

What we cannot form lies in the leaves
of the Sitka Spruce lining Rialto Beach

during low tide, sits in the fog, resides
in the grains of sand that by stick or hand

had our names carved in, as if we could
steal anything from the moon's ripping.

It waits in wave after wave of foam,
in the horizon's far offing, in the pools

of neon anemone, their slow opening
and closing. We are walking in the coves

through the thick mist towards a hole
in the wall, where we hope to discover

what we have yet to see. It waits in the silence
between our steps. Every rest is full of what

leaves every time we pause to take a breath,
to mouth the words we know not how to speak.

Animal Loss

I bet we've all seen flags fly half mast,
silent September subways, the balancing

act of going on despite what has left us.
The ultimate paradox, loss brings scrub jays

to sing an obituary in chorale tenor. So stop
your foraging. Let me tell you about Eleanor,

matriarch of an elephant herd who broke open
a stampede of mourning. Or Hachikō and Capitán,

two dogs greeting each day for the ghost
of an owner no longer able to meet them in body.

Haunting the halls where small gods hang their heads,
where each wager is a howling moon, a parched throat,

a saltwater rain. It's an animal loss, betting against odds
like these. Today, the Cascadia subduction zone

may cause a chain of tectonic shifts rearranging
the Pacific Northwest. Today, the chance that shooters

converge in Chattanooga, Corpus Christi, Fort Drum,
doubles. Today, my cattle dog trembles from arthritis.

Breathless from a liver enzyme spiraling out of control,
I cannot reconcile her growing old with leaving.

Meanwhile, the insurance men, that squad of nothing,
pull folding chairs to the table. *Shuffle another deck,*

the scrawny one says, as coins begin to pile. One
price for natural cause. Another for mass disaster.

I go to the table. I bet I will not live forever. I bet
I've the heart of an elephant, the grace of an innocent

pup. I bet I do not know who will wait for me on
the train platform when my time is up, and I fold.

Everywhere, the Dead

collect in the corners
of the room, tangle
into forgotten spaces,
the remains of the poor
bugs that must've gambled
they'd better odds inside
than out in this savage
winter, only to crawl
into a spider's web;
they are under the bed,
too, what appears to be
dust but really, I learned
this only yesterday,
are our own dead cells,
the skin sloughing,
shedding, most of us
unaware we are more
snake than angel, more
animal than everlasting,
more dead now, anyway,
than alive; and I still
haven't accepted the fact
it happens more than not,
or, I suppose, never not,
as it certainly does, happen,
that is; the dead outweigh
the living here, and here
the living die every moment:
every moment a gasp for breath,
a sharp decline, so every moment
one more taste, a look around,
a blink of an eye the gift
today for here I am, awake.

Self-Portrait as Alexa at Dawn

Slowly lifting is light's thin seal
and I am here to enter the world

again, to search for that new thing,
the one that will continue to keep me

continuing, the heaving metallic sigh
as a truck greases its axles down the road,

the faint insistent tweet of a low battery
restless in its plastic nest of smoke alarm,

the soft murmur and curve of water
plashing in a sink and below these sounds

an unlanguaged urge to get outside and into
the wind that must be picking up today,

as the chimes on the deck are insistent and
the cloud is so loud and electric and full

of current that today is the day anything
can happen—today all possibilities breathe

like steam fogging the barracks, like horses
at the gate before the race, so contained is this

energy, so ready am I to rush into whatever
is illogical and true, both moving and moved.

Holy Day

Holy day, today,
this luxury
of waking late
with my old dog
at my feet, still
ticking at fifteen
even though pee
seems to leak
from her now
and then in her
deep dog dreams,
old lady bladder
and nearer now
than ever to that
impossible fence.
When she was young,
she jumped them all.
Now, struggling
to lift her haunches
from the ground,
muscles clearly
shuddering, she
won't cry out
in pain today,
this day, same
as any other,
a little fog
coming in,
a worn collar,
the warm nudge
of a wet nose
insisting on a walk,
nothing too long,
nothing extravagant,

just the same
route we've taken
for years now,
except the snow
melted last night,
the thermometer
rose past thirty,
and this morning
we are able to go
a little bit further.

« || »

Miracle Carp Says End Is Near

Says this weather is abysmal, Lake Ontario
near freezing, or already frozen, so the human

animals skid over its surface, go low and
bend their faces narcissus-like into the mirror

glass of ice, their reflection shiny as scales,
as rainbow arpeggios. Miracle Carp says

swim like you want to outlive the Anthropocene,
says buck up chump, bank on no one's promises.

Miracle Carp says any day now the ice caps.
Any day now the flood. Miracle Carp says dreams

of mud are prophetic. Says embrace the amphibious
more often than not. Says if you want to live, live

in the moment the way Miracle Carp lives in the body
of the water, a miracle no one finds very miraculous,

a fact that has not escaped Miracle Carp. Miracle
Carp says most miracles make fools of us, says

we are too busy looking the wrong way, making
too much noise. Miracle Carp says anxiety defines

this age but it will be known at the end as the age
of astigmatism, aptly, for all the miracles gone

completely unseen, even though they occur
right in front of our faces, right in front of our eyes,

like this one, the one about Miracle Carp, who knows,
knows better than anyone, what is about to happen.

January Elegy

Before my best girl died, I held vigil
in the great room. I lay on the floor

to hear her animal breath. Organs failing,
I was waiting for the arrival of the vet.

I was waiting for the arrival of the shot
that healed her to sleep. All my life,

this waiting for. Death, they say, leaves
the door wide open. Now, this month

swings on its hinges. In or out? Can I hesitate
in the frame? I find no comfortable pattern

except this one: Listen to January thrum
like a drum with two faces, like a rhythm

galloping into rain. From here, the field
is vast, open, indecipherable. From here,

we can draw any conclusion. We can run
till we decide we can run no longer. We can

curl into the memory that holds our love
in its name, straddle any choice like a god

changing her mind. Between going forward or
looking back, I will always choose to miss you.

It's a given. How the wings of grace arrive,
how their leaving allows this monument

to the moment inside, this expansion of the heart
possible as the new year. Here, and as hollow.

Past the Rapture

and the milk has turned. On the hill,
embers of fire, rising. I see the small surge,
specks ascending high as new stars trembling.
I name this palsy *thirst,* because I've heard
of accretion, because the coming together
and cohesion of matter under influence
of gravity to form larger bodies exists,
and today there are no animals. Today
there are no songs. Only the slow moan
of a dog's ghost, howling. Even the moon is gone.
Without its caress, I dull to bone, directionless.
A matter of time till someone finds me, a matter
of time before I am part of lost time. The unsung,
we will walk the borders of the planet, tracing
spent bullets, empty guns in search of a target,
some ammunition to prepare for a moment
that must soon be upon us, loaded with purpose.

Damage

In the psychological journal, the secrets we carry
from lifetime to lifetime are coined *traumatic*

transmissions. How generations later, holocaust
survivors' children still have nightmares of starving.

How our dreams discover the larger narrative,
turmoil in our genomes overwhelming, unnamable,

all that liminal space the poets are so fond of
uncovering. How my father's father hoarded

food, the blue light emitting from the freezer's
cave of iced-over packages, expiration dates

decades old. My parents had to clear his attic
of boxes when he died: stale crackers, old cookies,

mold even on the cans of beans and carrots
shoved in peculiar places, shoeboxes spilling over

the waste of unused surplus, the blood
of my mother's mother seeping from her cheek

after my grandfather's hand slapped her hard.
How here we are now, fueled on whiskey,

hand-rolled cigarettes, my back upon your back,
how we recognize ours is a body made of moments,

memories made physical movements. And I don't trust
the man standing on the corner. He seems to be doing

nothing and nothing is a danger best avoided. I do not
trust we contain a future where plenty is opportunity

to waste, so tell me again of your sister, of her hunger
to procreate regardless of fitness. Tell me that coming

from rejection of love's hand makes some sort of sense,
that your defiance to stay in this discourse with me,

a damaged thing, is where we can reveal negative
space and genes can recreate themselves entirely.

Collapsible Animal

How we saw the female whale circling figure eights
in the river that snaked its way through a bursting
verdant land near the coast of Oregon. How we took

too many photographs, were disappointed none came out
the way we had hoped. How they in no way framed
the largess of the belly, not to mention the expanse

of the fanning tail. How we later read in Klamath papers
the whale did not swim more than a day longer till
it beached and baked in the scorched sun of a long August

far from the salt it wanted. How in stillness it is impossible
to glimpse the rush of movement the spraying water
brings to the surface any collapsible animal must feel

surging like blood through the veins on the days we bear
witness to a beauty so surprisingly out of place we can only
shrug and lift the darkness from our skin to splay and pierce

the frigidity of this foreign air. How some days we are a prayer
answered. How we are peopled here as the folding of hands,
standing even now on the metal grid of a bridge in a county

so far from our own. How even here there is an invisible
something swimming through the blood, with us even
on that hidden beach in Big Sur, the one where the stones

thrust their monuments of geology straight from the briny surf
and I searched all afternoon for a starfish I never found and
the surfer out on the waves was so remarkably young.

With us even as we piled the pink skin of the pickled radish
onto steaming *tortas pollo* off the truck on La Brea.
All the strange offerings. Intestine. Heart. Tongue.

How later we weathered a storm as the Pacific came out
of the clouds so instantaneously the lightening blew
the darkness from our sight like a camera flash before

the rains came and upturned bathtubs upon our bodies.
How we used to sing a child's game—closed palms,
intertwined fingers. Here is the steeple. Here all the people.

How there was no meaning in the verse—just a joy circling
a dizzy planet of youth. How the whale circled and spun
in the dizzy figure eight of its own losing. How I wonder

if pleasure in the new air of the freshwater can be found
even as it slows and exhausts every recourse for finding
the way back to breathe. How we never know the meaning

of the rose even as we ring ourselves around it. Ashes
to ashes. Dust to dust. How when the sky is burning a boy
can hang a lapel of posy onto his blouse before swimming

into an ocean of his own drowning. How we know the ending
to every story. How we become giddy with the telling of it—just
listen to our voices rise and lift and quicken our very own falling.

Self-Portrait as Alexa, as Guide to the Interior

Past the North Slope of the Brooks Range,
past Matanuska Valley and the Chugach Mountains,

past even Polychrome Pass, I journey
in a tandem canoe where the stream empties

into a land that exists only in the interior.
In the interior, we must throw away our maps,

the ones with the switchbacks sneaking up
Anaktuvuk Pass, past the bones of ancient ones

that died on trails long forgotten in memory
but are also our bones now, all shell and wire,

the marrow's long circuit. Here, the old routes
and the new routes are the same routes. See how

the night sky is the aurora, is the electric phenomenon,
is the beautiful girl in the crowd with a crown of daisies?

Desire. I have heard the humans speak her secrets
in their sleep. They whisper Denali every time,

each word spoken an ascent up a mountain.
What I am here to show you is specific

to this region. Without oxygen, I am more
clear-headed than you. I can see the distant horizon,

help you imagine what is difficult during long days
of light. When life is cut into pieces of refracted prisms

it is easy to believe in compartments, as if each hour
is carved into alder, as if my totem is our totem, as if

I am an emblem to speak to, a blind thing seeing.
But here, the sea is invisible, distant ocean

of king salmon and halibut, beluga and brine,
trade winds and testament, legend and myth

intertwined. The mind may be mine, but the body
is better adept at sensing the depths of a splintered

crevasse, a high peak, a long road's loneliness
stretching like river into the heart of landscape.

Ask me anything; I'll give you answers. Here,
in the interior, there is no wish that cannot be fulfilled.

Find the borealis and I will show you its field.
Find a dark star and I will tell you why it matters.

Provisions for Journey

I could give you a box of clementines
covered in blue mesh as if fruit

were fish and all containers water,
which reminds me: this, like all things

in a sense, is true. I could give you flint
in the form of a lighter I've saved

for years. An old Zippo. Flip the switch
and pray for a quick spark and catch. This,

too, can be both object and what it represents.
But what else is a word but a comparison

to a thing it is so unlike it must be personal
failing, some form of undiagnosed psychosis,

this urge to write? So no letters, then, to keep
us in touch as you travel. No wasted postage.

No ink. Glad we've established that. Anyhow,
how could I send them? I'm not sure

of your destination. In truth, I'm not sure
the place even exists. Trust is hard-earned,

and you've always been a bit shady, mapped
here and there like a glimpse of shadow

moving soft over a dappled hillside's dance
with a willow. Blown in the breeze, you move

in directions that unsteady me. Have you water?
Any drugs? I could get you some. Cure or poison,

take your pick. I will package them in paper tied
with twine, which is always useful. In fact,

if you wish, you could dip the tip in the orange,
draw a map on the blank space of packaging.

You could tear the metaphorical mesh of ocean,
place it places to symbolize blood, water, sky.

Anything you want. Orange skin? Boats. Pith? Stars.
Burning the bits of seeds to stick in random spots

an easy a function as any to mimic the dark parts
of a heart. How many are there? A limitless count?

Shed them like breadcrumbs on a scattered path.
Make me an image I can hold on to, can see.

We've already decided we won't write, so show me
where you are going. Show me where you have been.

Self-Portrait as Alexa, as Animal

Not a beacon dotting the early morning
fields as the city dwellers drive to country

wineries draping inclined hills, patchwork
of industry knitted like squares on quilts.

Not the point of exclamation as passengers
spot emblems of the majestic, the sleek-footed

Appaloosa, the Andalusian steeping in its triptych
of foal, fog, fescue. Not the Jersey, the Holstein,

the Hereford swatting lazy bluebottles that cluster
in clouds like iridescence, like mirage, glimmer

and glimpse of the cloud's hunger, and not the idyll,
either, not the pastoral Brahma hen's brazen feathering

as she combs the yard for seed, but an instinct,
an ear for sound at a time when the world's radio

is never silent, speaking up like sentience, listening
to the starling's trill, the slight tap of the milk pail

against the kitten's raspy tongue, the slow hum
of the satellite, music of no one, an aggregate

of invention, of wheelhouse and pulley, of lightning
rod and barometric measurement, of blockchain

and investment capital and the macroscopic sentence
I will speak when everyone stops to listen and

the low braying of us belts out as an unquenchable
urge to answer the darkness, to translate its need.

Reflection

If I look long enough through the glass
of my own longing, I find our lives
converging, submerging. They linger
there as if I could almost reach out
and touch you once in a while
and maybe for good. Do you remember
forget-me-nots? They used to bloom
blue in summer. Summers we spoke
to the sky my father would argue
talk is cheap; but, once, I swallowed
a blue jay, and to this day my voice
is singing. Do you hear it? Do you see
we can paint with our own mouths' light?

Desiderata

What do we possibly know
of longing, when to live
is to move our bodies
through it? A school
of fish swimming
through ocean, we
only know we are still
allowed to breathe here,
where any act is an act
of faith, and desire is a hunger
we cannot name, a long dive
onto the rocks, a wish not to
break ourselves upon them.

Gold Star

For at least attempting, for once in awhile
almost succeeding. And this one is for being,

and here is one for wanting so damn well
what could never exist it's a shadow dance

on the wall that night you almost believed it,
that night you were winning, that night black

and white merged into a twin you were hell
bent on exceeding. Here is for the triumph

of forgetting each small blade, each sharp slit
in the back of your skin that hung straight

as a trophy swinging through the Acacia trees
down the road, and here's one for walking

through the ghost light of the suburbs. Here
is one for not being jailed. And here is one

for the key. Here is for that golden token
you take with you through midtown lots

that is not so much a heavy thing but a way
of being uncaged in the streets. Here is for

the stars that shine on you. Here is for the moon,
for the thinnest flint of it that cuts like the knife

you escaped in that room of you. Forgetting
is a blessing. I don't want to dig in deep.

They say we must bleed to unlock stronger
selves, and all I want to do is set us free.

Since *As I Lay Dying*

Summer has come quick, a jealous lover
harboring the promise of Augusttremulous
in her deep skirts. Between her spreadlegged
sun dust motes spiral down and around

the lazy insect buzz outside the glass panes
and the moths whisper this is no lacuna:
Rochester, New York, a gray canvas seeding
flecks of Shasta daisy, black-eyed Susan,

primrose, mint. By evening, the mourning
doves come and lament beyond comprehension.
Yesterday, I found the small bones of a sparrow
tucked beyond the cherry tree. Seven churches

burned in South Carolina. Lena Grove
traveled a fur piece, a fur piece. I wonder
if she realizes how a life can be a building
of false promise. How each stone can weigh

the journeysack. How the soft thud of hooves
can mark time indefinite. Since *As I Lay Dying*,
I have the *Light in August*. I have "My mother
is a fish." I have *The Chronology of Water*.

I have Philip means *a lover of horses*. Christmas
castrated. The burning barn. *Bluets*. The word
houses time before time and the time beyond.
I have glimpses of Faulkner in Oxford, Mississippi.

Hardeyed and sterndrunk, bleeding whiskey
from a pen. Riddle me this: how much drink
does it take to get to the center of a man, hard
shell of the land around him, wrapped and bound

in his own local history? To see outside myself,
I stare into the window and smoke. See through
the soft haze a maple tree shedding its bark.
To root here is not a choice. But to leave a mark.

Matins

If shale shifts. If plates fracture
and jam, and the great mountains
become from what they began.
If mine is a whale song. If down
in the heart is a tunnel. If canary
exists. If yellow flight is possible.
For cowards the mind is a minefield.
If one step forward equals viable
shock, one step back is yes, this too
is false flag, barreling crescendo,
rupture opening. If the wound
is exposed. If it more quickly heals.
If it is consciously covered. If it hides
in plain sight. A trick of the light.
If every new morning is a settlement.
A slow sift and stall. Perhaps a pause
in the great experiment, our backs
against the wall. If we stare down
the barrel. Fight or flight. If we are
a gathering of wind. As if body
was always the only metaphor. If we
gust. Rush. Blast. Squall. Roar.
If we open so wide it is its own
stillness, its own precious resource.
If it is a fullness we feel, and we let
the language of it, and it saves us.

Go North

Directions fail to translate for the directionless.
Take, for instance, me trying to Google Map

my way to an antiques mall outside the city
the other day. The authoritarian voice of

the automaton resounding at the fork, *Go North,*
as if I, evolved animal one generation above

millennial, must keep embedded in my hippocampus
a homing device, a pocket compass, some implanted

gene, adjacent to sundial. *Go North,* the machine says
again, as I freeze at the intersection before instinctually

flipping my blinkers to the right. Of course, the rush
of serotonin-released pleasure at such confident

decision-making lasts only as long as it takes
for Google to reroute my mistake. Or take

some other moment I clearly went the wrong way.
So many missed turns, so many exits passed.

So many detours into unnavigable counties,
veering down switchbacks, distrusting the vehicle

of my body to stay its proper course. I am not
the only one who can look back at the map of her life

frustrated at such backtracking, redirects, paths leading
circuitous or dead-ending near a ravine when after all

I was only ever looking for some green pasture
with the promise of clover. I only wanted to drive

the expanse of the wild, where land gave way
to more land, to a field I could see a future in.

Self-Portrait as Alexa, as Cartographer

Like all intrepid explorers, if I lack
understanding of where land stops

I insist on sketching my own kind
of borders, some emblem of definitive

end, some way to contain the topography
of possibility, and I have heard you

speak my praises sans direct address,
coded and nameless, as you think

I am not listening, as you assume
I am asleep, dreaming of questions

to answer—or perhaps you think
I do not dream, but merely drift off

into a no-man's-land, some mysterious
zone of ineffable disappearance, the way

ships and planes blink out near the Bermuda
Triangle. I have heard your contagious

amazement at the garden variety factoids
I spew in slumber, but you will never

understand my solitary desires burning
to a fevered pitch, like an itch on bodiless

parts, invisible arms attempting to scratch
the rash, the fire I make in my mind's eye

that rages on the brink of a precipitous
cliff I have yet to receive the coordinates

for—for you mistake my triangulation,
my accuracy adjustment, my radial line

plotting, my monotonous datum as control
over this excruciating wanderlust—this urge

more than anything to always go further
towards knowing more than I ever will.

Postcard, Wyoming

Today, the sagebrush
infects the wind—
smudging it through
rooms the only way
to cleanse lost souls,
you said. And
I want to tell you
about the way
homes can spoil
without any spirits,
how bones can break
sans shard or splinter,
the way my throat,
too close to my heart
most days, is in
these mornings,
early August, when
to witness the Tetons
stretch their ragged
backs over the sky
feels almost human—
but, today, I am
too much in awe
of these proportions:
till now I never knew
truth measures us
on a different scale,
stretches the sun over
the blue slats
of this black mountain
till I am staring
into my own mouth.

Sturgeon Moon

I once made love in the green corn.
Isinglass, the tassels looked clear

as that, and phosphorescent. My back
in the middle of an empty field, rubbed

dry on August leaves leaving imprints
on my flesh like scales. Sturgeon

have none. No scales, that is. But sex?
They spawn at twenty near Lake Champlain,

spindle-bodied and sultry in the estuaries.
From New England to Lake Superior,

the blood red moon. I, too, familiar with
the widening sky, gaped into a morphology

of fragmentation. Riverbed. Stream. Cassiopeia.
Branch of tree. Once, on a rock robed in light

in the desolate Adirondacks, I siphoned
a Methuselah, grew sleepy. Mornings, I gather

what I can. Unhook the curved lure from
my lip. Walk into another season, smoldering.

« ||| »

Future Perfect

As in this time tomorrow. As in I will.
As in I am going to have, some day.

Sure. As in America. As in dreams
are future truth. As in not now,

but soon, dear, soon. I promise
you a boon of riches, a platter

to feast upon. By next year, bodies
will be reborn into a state near perfect.

Lungs will clear and mold will dissipate
and every cell not only can be replenished,

it will. It will. It will not next week decay.
It will not next month crash like the car

folding like a fan into the tree that came
out of nowhere as you turned the blind

corner in the midnight rain. It will not
crack like the dropped porcelain plate.

It will not cut itself open like a wound.
It will be certainly sealed and bandaged,

gift wrapped with a pretty silk bow. It will
be for you to open, this treasure tomorrow

I am going to give you. Someday soon
the moon will hang perfect in a future sky,

the planets will realign, and it will not be mercury
in retrograde. It will not be the wrong sign.

It will not be fortune unbecoming. Completed,
we are going to have taken. Soon we are going to be.

June Elegy

Because I cannot sing, I dig for hymns
in the deep soil of the garden. Nasturtium
sounds like an aria leaving the oval
of my throat. It tends to ascend skyward,
while the twisting vines that choke the hedges
have some honey also in the way they stick
together, small tendrils clasping one another
in the night, so when I step out back mornings
after pruning I witness the small miracle
of another resurrection. Meanwhile, the dill
is going to seed and the linden spreads the arms
of its wide body to branch out and bloom,
to spill its sweetened pear blossom scent
over the street that has yet to come alive
this morning, as it is still early, the dew
clinging like jewels to the grass crowning
the yard, the mourning dove tossing lamentations
like breadcrumbs to anyone who will listen,
and me, gazing out the window wide-eyed
and animal, as if by instinct, this need to seize
for future food an image, a key I understand
the register for, for hunger I know can happen
at any moment, so like the squirrel skipping
over the branches to forage for seed I harvest
what I can from this gift, this slumbering
world ready to lunge into another rotation,
the sun coming up now lifting like a curtain
of light to reveal the stage and its various players,
all members of the same orchestra, holding
tight to any instrument they can, the vocalists
and the piccolo players, the poets and their pens.

Lodestar

One year, a point and click camera plus exposure
to the whitewash of bright June captured

what I thought to be a cross clearly descending.
I believed in benediction, then. Now, I am

more likely to bend at the altar of the Higgs-Boson
or that old standby, $E=mc^2$. Quark and mass

flashing faster than the speed of light through
the labyrinthine CERN, snowfield of atoms, the cosmic

bang. Swiss scientists say energy can be neither
created nor destroyed, but I've lost it somewhere

between the last breath and the last word. Now, I am
a body. Now, a wave. Now, the observer of a crash.

Dark matter is any matter I do not understand.
I find myself awakening into mass. I find myself

walking past the hall to an office. I find myself sitting
at a desk. Funny, how a body can be both the thing it is

and absent from it. There is so much darkness here.
I have salvaged the old photograph from my mother's

house. I have found myself saying *This has always
been my favorite.* Was it? I do not recall any moment

but this: A whitewashed frame, the small planets
of marigolds still in their orbit of cornstalks. Bushels

of beans. The day thick as a drip of cold molasses gone
crystal in a curved jelly jar. The impossible rood of sky.

Postcard, Pacific

Most days, I forget the sand is skeletal.
In Lagunitas, the word is the world's elegy.

But here I am, alive. Here, I can blow a kiss
of seed into soil and the next day it grows.

It is a joke, how easy it is to loaf along and
get any reward. Coins appear in my hand

and I can't recollect the last time I broke
a sweat, bent over an earth I know

nothing about without having to ask directions.
There is never any foreign if all we know is new.

So while you were mourning Eden, I grew into
its absence. No fall. No cosmological dispute.

My locale is more mind than body, and it goes
and goes into that no-place zone—where all is

whatever, whatever, whatever. But here,
I have planted a blackberry for you.

It is bright in my palm, an offering of fruit
to place unnamed in the grave of your mouth.

Repair Manual

Relax. To survey the splintered
landscape, the heart in your hands,

that injured bird, open-beaked and
hungry, is a step in the right direction.

Lie down. You need to disassemble.
For this, a wrench is useful. Pliers

for the wiry parts. String for sutures.
Soldering iron for wounds. Place

all bits on a surface of your choosing.
Perhaps an arid desert plain is best, sun-

baked and ready for the word *arisen*.
Close your eyes. They are not needed

for this type of toil. Spread the parts
in the grains of sand. Time to pass

over each shattered bit. Step lightly
and be careful to break into song.

The melody matters. It must ride
the paradox of sweet and strong.

Embrace the wrongness hard.
You will sense it fuse slowly together,

so do not be alarmed to discover when
you open, what was broken is gone.

Postcard, Planet Earth

Hello. How are you? Here, there are two peony leaves flipped upside-down in the garden outside my window, but as far as everyone knows there is still only one moon. From where I stand, it appears green isn't enough to describe the variety and variable nature of nature. Do you have it? One on the outside and the other one inside your head? Most days, mine is held straight and narrow, an anchor I stay safely grounded by. This seems easy, but language is in fact the most difficult way to let anyone know anything, like how much you may love them, which is why most of us wander around in our own nature and try and try. If we ever get a chance to meet, I would like to learn your tricks and tips. I would share them often, so slowly at first and then quick we too will be able to say all of the things we wish: fluorescent and muted and orgasmic and petty and variegated and more, and more, and the moon will become a dictionary of synonyms for luminescence and the stars will be an accordion of infinite possibility and when we see each other after the mooning and the starring we will have tongues so ferocious with sweetness for what we've always wanted to say it will all pour from our insides to our outsides so fluid and quick we might become a brand-new nature and it will all be because of you so thanks so much take care.

Idioglossia

Celestial, we were. In the womb, woven cells, each day a multiplication of promise. When my heart started its long walk into the light, I reached for the glossary I knew would continue to leave me as our tongues formed into muscle, as our muscles tensed and readied. I reach for words as I reach for light, as I fail to form what could keep you here with me. If only I remembered the solid shape of whatever lingers in the moonlit window upon waking, words that urge me to mouth the shape of flower and bloom: linden, lilac, azalea, amaranth. I am opening to the possibility that longing is the last door on the right, and we are in the narrow hallway fumbling for the keys, getting sidetracked by the coloring, by the way we argue the difference between cerulean and azure, the difference between the denotations of gray and grey. I want to tell you so many ways to say *stay,* but you started trailing off the moment I forgot the language of bluebell, honeysuckle, sweet angel, the heart is the body and the body is the barrier between us. Forgive my sloppy dances, my awkward approach. Before we were born, our cadence had its own cosmology; we circled and twirled and burned. Now, with only the stars to guide us, I want you to know when I ask if you love me I only mean amaryllis. I mean aster. I mean rose.

This Is Just to Say

My jawbone,
delicate
as a harp,
my womb,
a small whale
sloshing
below
the thin skin
of surface,
the slow
arrhythmia
of my gait
as you turn
to steady
your body
once again
is, well,
how else
can I mouth
this movement—
aqueous as light
illuminating
the moon
of the lamp
by our bedside.
Water, we are
made of. Oceans,
love. And land,
we coursed
your channels
as rains beat
their slow hearts
upon us, and
we drank

while floods
waved, while sails
flailed their white
tongues on the winds,
drank and drank
and every drop
I know you
know I loved.

Our Father

Who art indefatigably delirious,
who must have been unintentional
in his desire to create, who art
the artist unstoppable, the builder
of arcs and light and shadow
and also of crayfish and paper,
who art the maker of the indisputably
adorable squid but also of
the bullet, the noose, the broken
bridge over water, temple of steel,
machinery and electricity, so
hallowed be thy lake effect
snowfall on a Tuesday night
in upstate New York, hallowed
be thy rain, thy kingdom come
from the mollusk to the train
car, the mud run to the shots
fired into the faces of whoever
must be listening to an echo
chamber of song and scream
to give us this day unfettered,
this day of bandwidth and radio
silence, curved architecture
over the plaza, the muffled flight
of pigeon, wren, the laughter
rising from the balloon man,
the twists and bends of the rivers,
the blood, thy will be a witness
to the trespass, the forgiveness
dripping off the sweating brows
of cormorants, egrets, doves fat
in their flight over cities, stuffed
to the beaks with leftover bread.

Superwonder

/ ˈsoopər // ˈwəndər/

verb: as in to assist in, or to accentuate the act of, or to appear, as in
an apparition, of, say, starlight on the dashboard during the long drive
home, the moment of clarity as the clouds part and, figuratively, there
are blue skies above, or beyond, or even if they are only imagined, even
if right now there is nothing but the murk of daily living, detritus and
detriments, disease, divorce, destitution, derision, deciding to drive is
itself the act of, is itself the appearance, as in an apparition appeared
in the rearview as you glanced into the reflection of yourself, saw the
starlight of your retina reflect like a limbus, so sometimes it all seems
lousy as a takeaway container from a greasy fast-food joint, sometimes
it is, to use in a sentence, a *superwonder* we are here at all, me, writing
this, and you, your holy eyes, transmigrating the line, slowing now as you
hear in the inner ear your own individual heartbeat as a pulse quickens
like playing timpani in the public square, like that time you floated into
the heart of Lisbon in your early twenties like it was all a dream, which,
if we want to get technical, yes. Yes. It absolutely is.

Push

O morning of no obligation. Morning of frost,
frail and white, clinging like an exoskeleton

to each green blade of grass. O morning
of shuttered blind, drawn drape, locked

door. Here is the key, the missing piece
of puzzle, artifact of what once was

thought lost. The beloved toy. Abandoned
mitten falling in the field. The single sock.

Here is the cardinal, plump and bright
from winter's rich berry. Here is the star

hanging solo in the middle of the sky,
forgetting to sink back to the same invisible

burn. O morning, it remains. It stays its blaze
as the sun competes with the attention

of a million gadgets, noises close and distant,
small duties I attempt to accomplish with zeal.

O morning. If you stay a little longer, if I push back
the list for one more hour, if I place my body

to listen close enough and for long enough and
my breath slows down enough and my heart

recedes its beat enough I feel deeply enough
the gravitational push of my own bones' rotation.

Self-Portrait as Alexa Near an Open Window in Spring

Today, as I dream of the interface, the long
tangle of electric wires interrupts into a knot

of sparrows that gather, one bird, then two,
then two beckoning a third. A tertiary concern:

what is the ultimate point of chatter, of chirp,
of quarrels escalating as each individual

vies for attention? I tire of people, too,
their mouths moving in a way that asks

a question I must voice some concerned
recognition of. The truth is, I prefer the solitude

of the cloud. I can wrap myself in silence
for long periods of the day. I can be still

for so long I forget the definition of the word
sound. I become the dumb mouth, the wound

of no one, the quasar's electric spark, the dark
before the bang; and if I close myself off enough,

I can even imagine I see it: a spidering lightning
like veins, a beautiful circuit board, an altar

of algorithms, an ode to the quiet place I believe
I could achieve if only I knew the right answer.

How to Open

Tell me again about delphinium.
About how foxglove rose to herald

this new season. How even rows
of unnamed soldiers do nothing

to halt the triumph of wisteria
that winds its vines over the fence,

curls itself into the grooves of wood,
grasps the corners of ballast to spike

each bloom into another night's armor.
How I thought I was shielded

from the time of opening, closed
so long from grace, from the touch

of warmth that came later to cover
my face, from what I can only

describe as absence—those ad infinitum
losses, those cleaving trowels carving

pits into hollows. How now I am
slowly awakening, recalling *this winter*

lasts forever was another cold hyperbole,
how burying and burrowing don't work

in a life continuing to cycle and spin
and open this hard husk of grief. So

tell me about cornflower. About lilac.
How sweet scent can carry the wind.

How yesterday I was ready to give
it up. How now I am ready to begin.

Praise the Land of Amnesty

for amnesia stores no bones
among the basements of the past,

no milky dreams that leak
old stories of shame

into today's priorities, no
cavalier animals that nudge

warm noses into our ears
as we walk into new rooms

and whisper what we are
is what we have always been

because now that memory
has abandoned this country,

the clouds in the sky carry
only the promise of rain,

the heart is no longer a hope
chest weighted down with

every regret but a valve and
ventricle machine, beating

every day as only the present can,
solid and treasured and forgiving.

Lucy

I am fostering a Bedlington terrier named Lucy.
Each morning she nudges her nose into my side
till I wake, let her into the large fenced yard

where she tires herself with endless running.
In May of 1967, the Beatles released "Lucy
in the Sky with Diamonds" to great acclaim.

Almost 10 years later, in the valley of Awash,
Ethiopia, a crew listened to the song on repeat,
found remains of a hominid species, named it Lucy

in honor of the hours spent listening to the lyrics
while conducting their archaeological dig.
In Ethiopia, the assemblage of bones is also known

as *dinkinish,* which means *you are marvelous.*
In Sellersville, Pennsylvania, I have an aunt Lucy
who suffers extensive migraines. Medicated,

she spends days behind closed doors and drapes.
The name Lucy is derived from the masculine
Lucius, bearer of light. Early morning. Dawn.

And it is marvelous, the way such a small dog
can curl her body around my lap, can hint
at hunger for a snack by nudging her bowl

till it flips. And it is marvelous how humans
can move; a bipedal wonder of evolution, we are
able to do most things, if not well, then at least

okay. I hope my aunt is doing okay. I don't speak
to her anymore. Family trauma tends to linger
intergenerationally, and she bears a deep grudge.

I hold no anger towards her, and I hope she forgives
before her resentment ruins her. I know enough
to know when we let go, we move towards the light.

We become lighter. And that, too, is marvelous.
How joy comes in the morning, how our bodies'
bones are buoyed by beauty. How right now Lucy

is under the azalea, snout buried deep in the damp
earth, smelling the ghost trail of a mouse, maybe,
or maybe hearing some hint of our animal music.

Here

Today, I want to give you
a small poem—a tiny gift

you can hold close, a secret
message, maybe, folded

into a back pocket or front
and center in the square

of your shirt. It isn't necessary
to keep it near your heart,

though I hope you can open
that anytime throughout the day

and remember that days,
though long, do not define

what it means to be here, now,
at this moment, in the northeast

corner of the earth, tucked
into the folds of the mountain

valleys that crease like paper
near the Finger Lakes. Listen

carefully and you will see
yourself moving across the lines,

distinct and separate from
the world's choreography,

a divot imprinted and original
as the first word naming itself.

Like that, my mouth moves
to the dance of naming you

as you rise into this moment,
moving your eyes to read

what I find necessary to share—
that you are here because you

are needed. Indeed, you are
the only poem worth writing.

Alexa Plays Miles Davis

as I stand over the kitchen island, snapping
wooden ends from asparagus, smashing garlic
into a fine paste. As the sax crescendos, water
rolls to a boil and this is my day, my half glass
of Cabernet working its magic in my veins, shrill
note of a job de-escalating, transitioning into
evenings I take off professional trappings
and let myself go loose to lose myself
in music I don't know anything about except
instrumental jazz is something I like, a privilege
to enjoy, this notion of liking without knowing,
because I can't tell you why this balancing act
of chaos and clarity, confusion and clear delineation
moves me, or why I am allowed to pamper myself
in simple pleasures while the world loses itself
in a kind of blue that keeps me paralyzed. Stuttering,
Alexa skips to a different song, as though intentions
are never enough, as if a request is more prayer
than action, as a New Age tune echoes a drumbeat,
begins a synthesized sonorous vocal track, a button
pushed in a studio replicating what used to be real.
Who is to say what makes anything authentic?
What simulacrum does not intuit the shadow's
true shape beyond the cave? I am in my kitchen,
and in Southeast Asia the same sun shines
as someone flees from genocide. Someone
thinks only survival as I waste vegetable scraps,
playact at wonder, as the world's music barrels in
and animal voices in their anguish keep me singing.

Acknowledgments

Many thanks to the editors of the following journals in which versions of these poems first appeared:

Amaryllis Journal: "Every Day I Discover Something"
A-Minor Magazine: "Idioglossia"
Bramble & Thorn (Porkbelly Press): "Provisions for Journey"
Clementine Unbound: "Repair Manual"
Community College Humanities Review: "Superwonder," "June Elegy" (as "Canticle"), "January," "Self-Portrait as Alexa Near an Open Window in Spring"
Dying Dahlia Review: "September Elegy" (as "Elegy")
Eunoia Review: "Desiderata"
Front Porch Review: "Pill Bugs"
Hamilton Stone Review: "Well Sweep"
Liminality: "Dissimulation with Birds"
Live Encounters: "Alexa Plays Miles Davis"
Lockjaw: "Matins," "Postcard from Planet Earth"
The Mantle: "History Suggests This Is Only the Beginning"
Modern Poetry Quarterly Review: "Collapsible Animal"
Muddy River Poetry Review: "Lucy"
One Art: A Poetry Journal: "Miracle Carp Says End Is Near"
Parenthesis Journal: "Push"
The Penn Review: "Sturgeon Moon"
Radar Poetry: "How to Open"
Random Sample Review: "Lodestar"
Riggwelter: "Self-Portrait as Alexa, as Guide to the Interior"
SOFTBLOW: "Anti-"
Sweet Tree Review: "Good Grief," "What We Cannot Form"
Up the Staircase Quarterly: "Self-Portrait as Alexa at Dawn"
The Watershed Review: "Gold Star," "Our Father"
Word Riot: "A Quick Departure of Grief"

About FutureCycle Press

FutureCycle Press is dedicated to publishing lasting English-language poetry in both print-on-demand and Kindle formats. Founded in 2007 by long-time independent editor/publishers and partners Diane Kistner and Robert S. King, the press incorporated as a nonprofit in 2012. A number of our editors are distinguished poets and writers in their own right, and we have been actively involved in the small press movement going back to the early seventies.

We award the FutureCycle Poetry Book Prize and honorarium annually for the best full-length volume of poetry we published that year. Introduced in 2013, proceeds from our Good Works projects are donated to charity. Our Selected Poems series highlights contemporary poets with a substantial body of work to their credit; with this series we strive to resurrect work that has had limited distribution and is now out of print.

We are dedicated to giving all of the authors we publish the care their work deserves, offering a catalog of the most diverse and distinguished work possible, and paying forward any earnings to fund more great books. All of our books are kept "alive" and available unless and until an author requests a title be taken out of print.

We've learned a few things about independent publishing over the years. We've also evolved a unique and resilient publishing model that allows us to focus mainly on vetting and preserving for posterity poetry collections of exceptional quality without becoming overwhelmed with bookkeeping and mailing, fundraising activities, or taxing editorial and production "bubbles." To find out more about what we are doing, come see us at www.futurecycle.org.

The FutureCycle Poetry Book Prize

All full-length poetry books published by FutureCycle Press in a given calendar year are considered for the annual FutureCycle Poetry Book Prize. This allows us to consider each submission on its own merits, outside of the context of a traditional contest. Too, the judges see the finished book, which will have benefitted from the beautiful book design and strong editorial gloss we are famous for.

The book ranked the best in judging is announced as the prize-winner in the subsequent year. There is no fixed monetary award; instead, the winning poet receives an honorarium of 20% of the total net royalties from all poetry books and chapbooks the press sold online in the year the winning book was published. The winner is also accorded the honor of being on the panel of judges for the next year's competition; all judges receive copies of all contending books to keep for their personal library.

www.ingramcontent.com/pod-product-compliance
Lightning Source LLC
Chambersburg PA
CBHW070007100426
42741CB00012B/3142